TEST
YOUR
IQ

TEST ◇ YOUR
INTELLIGENCE

TEST YOUR IQ

PHILIP J. CARTER & KEN A. RUSSELL

JOINT EDITORS OF THE MENSA UK PUZZLE GROUP JOURNAL

WARD LOCK

A WARD LOCK BOOK

First published in the UK 1992
by Ward Lock
A Cassell Imprint
Villiers House
41/47 Strand
London
WC2N 5JE

Reprinted 1992, 1993, 1994 (twice)

Distributed in the United States by Sterling Publishing Co., Inc.
387 Park Avenue South, New York, NY 10016-8810

Distributed in Australia by Capricorn Link (Australia) Pty Ltd
P.O. Box 665, Lane Cove, NSW 2066

British Library Cataloguing-in-Publication Data
A Catalogue record for this book is available from the British Library

ISBN 0 7063 7059 7

Printed and bound in Great Britain by Cox & Wyman Ltd, Reading

Contents

About the Authors

Kenneth Russell is a London surveyor and is also the Puzzle Editor of Mensa, the high IQ Society.

Philip Carter is an engineering estimator and also a Yorkshire JP. He is Editor of *Enigmasig*, the Mensa Special Interest Puzzle Group.

Acknowledgements

The authors are greatly indebted to their wives, both named Barbara, who, as well as supporting them enthusiastically in writing the book, have also contributed in compiling, checking and typing the manuscript.

Introduction

What is an IQ? The letters stand for Intelligence Quotient, and the definition of intelligence is 'the ability to comprehend quickly', while quotient is the number of times that one number will divide into another.

Thus, a child of eight years of age who successfully passed a test for a child of eight, but failed a test for a child of nine years would have an IQ of eight divided by eight, or 1 x 100 = 100, which would be the norm. A child of eight years of age, on the other hand, who successfully passed a test for a child of 10 years would have an IQ of 10 divided by 8, or 1.25 x 100 = 125.

With adults this method of calculation does not apply. They are judged on an IQ test of which the average score would be 100, and the results would be graded above and below this norm according to known test scores.

It is generally agreed that 50 per cent of the population has an IQ of between 90 and 110 per cent. Of the rest of the population, 25 per cent would be above, and 25 per cent below this mark.

Above this central group about 14.5 per cent of the population would have IQs of between 110 and 120; 7 per cent IQs of 120 to 130; and 3.5 per cent IQs of 130 and above.

Below the central group we find 14.5 per cent with IQs of between 80 and 90; 7 per cent between 70 and 80; and the remaining 3.5 per cent below 70.

Intelligence tests only measure a person's ability to reason. They do not measure other qualities that are required for success, such as character, personality, talent, persistence and application. A person with a high IQ only has a better chance of succeeding in life than a person with a low IQ if he or she applies his or herself to the tasks ahead diligently and with enthusiasm. Someone with a low IQ but with a high sense of achievement and great persistence could fare much better than a bright person.

Instructions

There are four complete tests numbered 1, 2, 3 and 4, and each test contains 10 parts, numbered with Roman numerals.

You have a limited time in which to complete the tests, so keep strictly to the time limit as this could affect your score, and work as quickly as possible.

Do not spend too much time on any one question. If you are in doubt, leave it and return to it using the time remaining. If you do not know an answer have an intuitive guess - you may well be right!

TEST ONE

Test One
PART I

Part 1 is a series of 20 questions designed to test your ability in collecting together objects or ideas that belong to a set or that have some common attribute. To make this classification simpler, we have put together a series of words and you have to spot the 'odd one out'. There are five words and only four of them have a common theme; underline the <u>odd one</u>.

Example: bag, basket, <u>hat</u>, pocket, bucket
Answer: <u>hat</u>; the other four are used for carrying things

You have 10 minutes to complete the 20 questions.

Each correct answer scores one point.

8-10	AVERAGE
11-13	GOOD
14-16	VERY GOOD
17-20	EXCEPTIONAL

1. cruise, holiday, voyage, passage, trip
2. foolish, audacious, stalwart, doughty, intrepid
3. ruse, artifice, ploy, action, subterfuge
4. house, residence, home, dwelling, building
5. snap, cut, crack, break, split
6. chip, mould, fashion, hammer, chisel
7. gazette, book, chronicle, newspaper, magazine
8. jumper, jacket, sweater, jersey, pullover
9. dig, scoop, delve, trough, gouge
10. burlesque, lampoon, jape, satire, parody
11. calm, quiet, relaxed, serene, unruffled
12. cerulean, vermilion, crimson, scarlet, carmine
13. dulcet, concordant, harmonious, euphonious, soft
14. big, tall, large, bulky, massive
15. duplicitous, ambiguous, deceiving, perfidious, two-faced
16. chicane, trick, deceive, insult, fraud
17. traitor, collaborator, enemy, quisling, betrayer
18. agrarian, urban, rustic, pastoral, bucolic
19. large, broad, pervasive, sweeping, widespread
20. zealot, admirer, fanatic, devotee, enthusiast

Part II is a series of 20 questions designed to test your knowledge of language and your ability to spot words that have the same meaning. We have grouped together five words, and from them you have to underline the <u>word</u> that means the same or has the closest meaning to the KEY word.

Example: ANGULAR (blunt, stiff abrupt, <u>branching</u>, cornered)
Answer: <u>branching</u> is the word closest in meaning to the KEY word, ANGULAR

You have 10 minutes to complete the 20 questions.

Each correct answer scores one point.

8-10	AVERAGE
11-13	GOOD
14-16	VERY GOOD
17-20	EXCEPTIONAL

1. HOPE (need, cheer, expectation, friendship, charm)
2. ABBEY (church, friary, building, cathedral, school)
3. PURPOSE (warrant, intention, nominate, interdiction, augur)
4. SLEEK (sinuous, glib, fast, long, lustrous)
5. WHEEL (pivot, complain, inveigle, stir, whinge)
6. DOVETAIL (meet, feather, weave, interlock, fan)
7. LUCID (timely, fruitful, sparkling, limpid, smooth)
8. GLOAT (win, crow, overwhelm, reward, rejoice)
9. RIPOSTE (blow, retort, fence, gamble, argue)
10. EBB (tide, low, calm, out, wane)
11. WHIMSICAL (capricious, charming, bizarre, happy, didactic)
12. GENTEEL (humane, creative, respectable, mild, natural)
13. DESIRE (enthusiasm, glean, flatter, expect, covet)
14. PAWN (knight, chess, puppet, piece, erotica)
15. PALL (hearse, jade, smoke, black, sallow)
16. COMPOSITE (combined, confident, constitution, calm, constituent)
17. CORROBORATION (enunciation, litigation, censure, proof, interaction)
18. COUNTERMAND (advocate, duplicate, retract, contradict, calculate)
19. FATHERLAND (Germany, country, parent, metropolis, history)
20. DEBILITATE (contend, weaken, puncture, execute, desecrate)

PART III

Part III is a series of 20 questions designed to test your knowledge of language and your ability to visualize opposite meanings quickly. We have grouped together five words, and from them you have to underline the <u>word</u> that means the opposite or is as nearly as possible opposite in meaning to the KEY word.

Example: CARELESS (exact, <u>heedful</u>, strict, anxious, dutiful)
Answer: <u>heedful </u>is the word that means the opposite of the KEY word CARELESS

You have 10 minutes to complete the 20 questions.

Each correct answer scores one point.

8-10	AVERAGE
11-13	GOOD
14-16	VERY GOOD
17-20	EXCEPTIONAL

ANTONYMS

1. SMART (dowdy, old, modish, ugly, putrid)
2. LIVING (ended, over, late, asleep, past)
3. DOUBT (sceptic, indubitable, disquiet, think, conviction)
4. PROFLIGATE (rich, chaste, bankrupt, slight, scanty)
5. PREDICTABLE (unreliable, awaited, unexpected, unknown, arbitrary)
6. OBVIOUS (blunt, distanced, obtuse, unsubtle, vague)
7. CAJOLE (wheedle, browbeat, inveigle, cold-shoulder, savage)
8. JOCULAR (apathetic, worried, solemn, angry, calm)
9. SLY (surreptitious, insidious, subtle, noisy, guileless)
10. VALIANT (withdrawn, introvert, craven, sneaky, unsuccessful)
11. FERAL (domesticated, soft, private, mindless, noble)
12. ROUTINE (hackneyed, confusing, exciting, abnormal, spatial)
13. LOATH (impassive, avid, wishful, brisk, content)
14. REGENERATE (change, stagnate, stop, hinder, destroy)
15. FUTILE (useful, erstwhile, vain, simple, calculated)
16. GAINSAY (gloom, forfeiture, damage, apathy, support)
17. SCRUPULOUS (fastidious, extravagant, reckless, moral, dangerous)
18. CULPABLE (blameless, wieldy, dull, liable, able)
19. LOYAL (perfunctory, pernicious, pertinacious, perquisite, perfidious)
20. EXPEDITE (admit, obstruct, diminish, relent, dismiss)

Part IV is a series of 20 questions designed to test your ability to visualize relationships between various objects and ideas. We have grouped together five words, one of which will pair up with the KEY word to produce a similar relationship to the two-word example. Underline the word that is appropriate.

Example: TIRED is to work as
HAPPY is to (sleep, rest, <u>success</u>, exercise, eating)
Answer: <u>success</u> has a similar relationship to HAPPY as work has to TIRED

You have 10 minutes to complete the 20 questions.

Each correct answer scores one point.

8-10 AVERAGE   11-13 GOOD
14-16 VERY GOOD   17-20 EXCEPTIONAL

ANALOGY

1. PINE is to tree as
   CUTLASS is to (steel, sword, weapon, gladiator, blade)
2. RESIGN is to politician as
   ABDICATE is to (throne, realm, prince, empire, king)
3. LAST is to penultimate as
   DECEMBER is to (month, January, winter, November, Christmas)
4. FRAGRANCE is to perfume as
   BOUQUET is to (incense, flowers, wine, soup, cooking)
5. NEURAL is to nerves as

RENAL is to (heart, kidneys, liver, lungs, back)

6. JEOPARDY is to peril as
   JEALOUSY is to (lust, envy, sin, insecurity, trust)

7. BARBED is to cutting as
   DEROGATORY is to (politics, insulting, perceptive, inappropriate, critical)

8. NURTURE is to neglect as
   DENIGRATE is to (extol, calumniate, reveal, recognize, want)

9. ORIGAMI is to paper as
   IKEBANA is to (fencing, trees, theatre, flowers, tapestry)

10. ISOSCELES is to triangle as
    SQUARE is to (rectangle, polygon, rhombus, quadrilateral, equilateral)

11. HOROLOGY is to time as
    DENDROLOGY is to (hair, plants, trees, teeth, soil)

12. EXCOMMUNICATE is to church as
    BLACKLIST is to (business, club, association, credit, veto)

13. PIPE is to conduit as
    LATTICE is to (cookery, trellis, decoration, wood, salad)

14. CHAIN is to saw as
    BOX is to (drill, knife, plane, chisel, spanner)

15. SPICK is to span as
    SWEET is to (talk, heart, potato, sour, meat)

16. FIRM is to flabby as
    PIQUANT is to (small, pleasant, large, salty, bland)

17. CASTOR is to furniture as
    ROWEL is to (spur, cage, bicycle, clock, hub)

18. LONGITUDE is to meridian as
    LATITUDE is to (degree, lines, tropics, freedom, parallel)

19. PITTANCE is to peanuts as
    PLATITUDINOUS is to (walnuts, stroppy, dish, corny, wishy-washy)

20. HYGENIC is to polluted as
    KNOWING is to (sagacious, misunderstood, secret, uncommon, ingenuous)

PART V

Part V is a series of 20 questions designed to test your knowledge of language and your ability to recognize quickly words of similar meanings. There are six words in each question and you have to find a pair of words that have similar meanings. Underline the <u>two words</u> that you believe to be the closest in meaning.

Example: <u>walk</u>, run, drive, <u>stroll</u>, fly, sit
Answer: <u>walk</u> and <u>stroll</u> are the two words in the list that are the closest in meaning

You have 10 minutes to complete the 20 questions.

Each correct answer scores one point.

8-10	AVERAGE
11-13	GOOD
14-16	VERY GOOD
17-20	EXCEPTIONAL

1. independent, manifest, explain, declaration, evident, multiple
2. sever, grind, whittle, shave, create, sheer
3. small, frail, old, puritanical, puny, worn
4. enrich, please, accept, provoke, delight, entreat
5. jaunt, visit, frolic, leap, excursion, tilt
6. mannerism, posture, virility, foible, method, story
7. derivative, imaginable, fanciful, plausible, prominent, clear
8. ripe, frugal, parsimonious, dreary, haughty, religious
9. diagonal, vague, parallel, square, linear, oblique
10. suggestion, slur, assertion, insinuation, remark, fall
11. rectangular, glib, pliant, muscular, gripping, flexible
12. stranger, miscreant, outcast, beggar, villain, mercenary
13. animal, beseech, prey, target, weapon, help
14. spoken, spontaneous, indelicate, sudden, profound, instinctive
15. discretion, strategy, tact, valour, firm, repute
16. scale, zero, spiral, cipher, vertex, pressure
17. sob, tramp, whim, complaint, vagary, dimness
18. aged, heavy, gloomy, scrupulous, calm, lugubrious
19. doubtful, hypothetical, untrue, assumed, actual, narcotic
20. traction, trail, grip, region, skill, impression

Test One
PART VI

Part VI is a series of 20 questions designed to test your knowledge of language and your ability to recognize words of opposite meanings quickly. There are six words in each question and you have to find a pair of words that have opposite meanings. Underline the <u>two words</u> that you believe to be opposite in meaning.

Example: curved, long, <u>big</u>, <u>small</u>, broad, fat
Answer: <u>big</u> and <u>small</u> are the two words in the list that are opposite in meaning

You have 10 minutes to complete the 20 questions.

Each correct answer scores one point.

8-10	AVERAGE
11-13	GOOD
14-16	VERY GOOD
17-20	EXCEPTIONAL

1. sorrow, animosity, anger, action, friendship, vitality
2. grand, old, fabulous, famous, charming, ordinary
3. fray, join, report, stretch, sever, twist
4. decline, abase, disagree, zenith, confide, glorify
5. stroke, stamp, wrinkle, shake, press, jiggle
6. normal, sane, singular, lonely, specific, chaste
7. bright, polished, civilized, smooth, theatrical, amateurish
8. credence, error, disbelief, religion, knowledge, sorrow
9. prescribe, heal, destroy, condition, operate, aggravate
10. offensive, kind, quiet, agreeable, ignorant, untrue
11. exiguous, direct, slow, meandering, doubtful, liberal
12. technical, mechanical, voluntary, systematic, manual, lifeless
13. adjacent, eccentric, erroneous, level, wayward, precise
14. rugged, diligent, critical, practical, indifferent, resolute
15. weak, specific, facile, sincere, difficult, unreal
16. frank, potent, mundane, rough, weak, small
17. fraternize, trust, shun, propose, distract, detract
18. honest, devout, unwise, unfriendly, sacrilegious, parsimonious
19. non-stop, unique, sporadic, slow, contrived, clever
20. suffrage, bondage, joy, obligation, ecstasy, emancipation

Part VII is a series of 20 questions designed to test your ability quickly to find alternative meanings of words. You are looking for a word that has the same meaning as one word or phrase in one sense and the same meaning as a different word in another sense. The dots represent the number of letters in the missing word. Fill in the missing word.

Example: breathes heavily . . . . . . underclothes
Answer: pants

You have 20 minutes to complete the 20 questions.

Each correct answer scores one point.

8-10	AVERAGE
11-13	GOOD
14-16	VERY GOOD
17-20	EXCEPTIONAL

DOUBLE MEANINGS

1. even-handed . . . . carnival
2. debris . . . . sailing vessel
3. fictional work . . . . . original
4. engage in conversation with . . . . opposite
5. container . . . jolt
6. target of ridicule . . . . large cask
7. piece of soft material . . . walk with soft tread
8. large bird . . . . . a shiny black colour
9. light blow . . . valve
10. deeply moved . . . . unnaturally mannered
11. throw or toss . . . . . machine part
12. benevolent . . . . genus
13. fruit seed . . . short high-pitched sound
14. a mark of damage . . . . craggy rock formation
15. burial chamber . . . . . bound
16. pat lightly . . . small flatfish
17. senior . . . . . tree
18. earth . . . . reduced to fine particles
19. walk with quick soft steps . . . . . . quick idle talk
20. clean or polish . . . . . look high and low

Part VIII is a series of 20 questions designed to test your ability at innovation. You are given the first part of the word or phrase, and you have to find the second part. The same second part then becomes the first part of a second word or phrase. The dots represent the number of letters in the missing word. Fill in the missing word.

Example: house . . . . all
Answer: hold

You have 20 minutes to complete the 20 questions.

Each correct answer scores one point.

8-10	AVERAGE
11-13	GOOD
14-16	VERY GOOD
17-20	EXCEPTIONAL

DOUBLE WORDS

1. question . . . . bodied
2. ear . . . . gun
3. life . . . . table
4. power . . . . . . work
5. counter . . . . post
6. just . . . cap
7. beg . . . self
8. tear . . . . out
9. short . . . . out
10. over . . . some
11. grim . . . tone
12. home . . . . bay
13. dust . . . tile
14. sport . . . . . word
15. villa . . side
16. play . . . chant
17. bed . . . . fall
18. air . . . . end
19. fish . . . work
20. upper . . . lass

PART IX

Part IX is a series of 10 culture-free tests designed to test your powers of logical reasoning and understanding of relationships, pattern and design. Study each display of diagrams and select the missing item from the choices given. Study the instructions given for each question.

Example:

You have 20 minutes to complete the 10 questions.

Each correct answer scores two points.

8-10	AVERAGE
12-14	GOOD
16	VERY GOOD
18-20	EXCEPTIONAL

1.

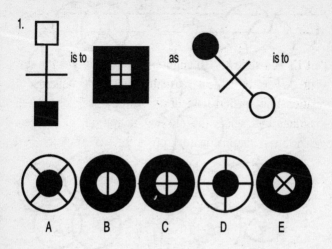

2.

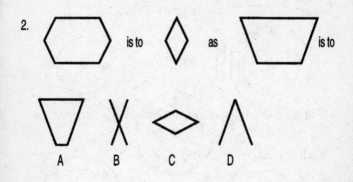

3. Which is the odd one out?

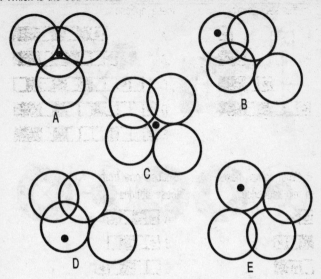

4. Which is the odd one out?

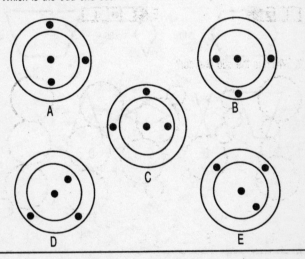

5. What comes next in this sequence?

Choose one from these options

A
B
C
D
E

6. What comes next in this sequence?

Choose one from these options

A
B
C
D
E

7. Which is the odd one out?

A   B   C   D   E

8. Which is the odd one out?

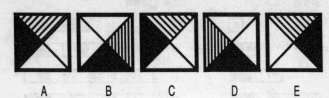

A   B   C   D   E

9. Which is the odd one out?

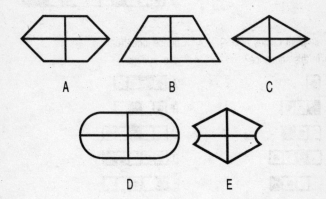

A   B   C

D   E

10. To which of the five boxes on the right can a dot be added so that it meets the same conditions as in the box on the left?

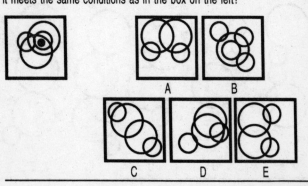

A   B

C   D   E

Test One
PART X

Part X is a series of 10 tests designed to test your powers of calculation and logic. From the alternatives given in each of the questions choose the answer that you think is correct.

Example: My watch shows the time at 12.25; one clock shows 12.10. The radio announces 12.30, the church clock strikes 12.00, and your watch shows 12.15. The correct time is 12.20. What is the average time, fast or slow, as shown by these timepieces?

A. 2 mins slow	B. 4 mins slow	C. 6 mins slow
D. 2 mins fast	E. 4 mins fast	F. 6 mins fast

Answer: B. 4 mins slow

You have 20 minutes to complete the 10 questions.

Each correct answer scores two points.

8-10	AVERAGE
12-14	GOOD
16	VERY GOOD
18-20	EXCEPTIONAL

1. Alf is half as old again as Jim who is half as old again as Sid. Their ages total 133. How old is Jim?

A. 30   B. 35   C. 36   D. 40   E. 42   F. 48

2. A car travels at a speed of 30mph over a certain distance and then returns over the same distance at a speed of 60mph. What is the average speed for the total journey?

A. 35mph   B. 38mph   C. 40mph   D. 42mph   E. 45mph   F. 48mph

3. How many minutes is it before 8am if 55 minutes ago it was four times as many minutes past 5am?

A. 15 mins   B. 20 mins   C. 22 mins   D. 25 mins   E. 28 mins   F. 35 mins

4. If the score on 8 dice totals 32, what is the average of the scores on the opposite sides?

A. 1   B. 2   C. 3   D. 4   E. 5   F. 6

5. A batsman is out for 10 runs, which reduces his batting average for the season from 34 to 32. How many runs would he have needed to score to increase his average from 34 to 36?

A. 52   B. 58   C. 60   D. 62   E. 66   F. 72

6. Five men competed in a 100 yard dash. Jim finished either 2nd, 3rd or 4th. Alf was not the winner. Sid finished one place behind Alf. Jack did not finish in second place. George finished two places behind Jack. Who finished in second place?

A. Jim   B. Alf   C. Sid   D. Jack   E. George
F. There is insufficient evidence to determine

7. What is the sum of all the numbers from 1 to 100 inclusive?
(i.e., 1+2+3+4+5 ... 96+97+98+99+100)

A. 3000   B. 3250   C. 4550   D. 4800   E. 5050   F. 7100

8. Jim has £3 more than Sid, but then Sid wins on the horses and trebles his money, which means that he now has £2 more than the original amount of money that the two men had between them. How much money did Jim and Sid have between them before Sid's win?

A. £9   B. £11   C. £13   D. £15   E. £19   F. £21

9. Sid's house is seventh from one end of the row and eleventh from the other end. How many houses in the row?

A. 15   B. 16   C. 17   D. 18   E. 19   F. 20

10. Out of 100 people surveyed 82 had an egg for breakfast, 80 had bacon, 65 had toast, and 78 had coffee. How many people, at least, must have had all four items - i.e., egg, bacon, toast and coffee?

A. 5   B. 6   C. 8   D. 11   E. 15   F. 17

Test One
ANSWERS

Part I
1. holiday 2. foolish 3. action
4. building 5. cut 6. hammer
7. book 8. jacket 9. trough
10. jape 11. quiet
12. cerulean 13. soft 14. tall
15. ambiguous 16. insult
17. enemy 18. urban
19. large 20. admirer

Part II
1. expectation 2. friary
3. intention 4. lustrous
5. pivot 6. interlock 7. limpid
8. crow 9. retort 10. wane
11. capricious
12. respectable
13. covet 14. puppet
15. jade 16. combined
17. proof 18. retract
19. country 20. weaken

Part III
1. dowdy 2. late
3. conviction 4. chaste
5. unexpected 6. vague
7. browbeat 8. solemn
9. guileless 10. craven
11. domesticated
12. abnormal
13. avid 14. stagnate

15. useful 16. support
17. reckless 18. blameless
19. perfidious 20. obstruct

Part IV
1. sword 2. king
3. November 4. wine
5. kidneys 6. envy
7. insulting 8. extol 9. flowers
10. quadrilateral 11. trees
12. business 13. trellis
14. spanner 15. sour
16. bland 17. spur
18. parallel 19. corny
20. ingenuous

Part V
1. manifest, evident
2. whittle, shave
3. frail, puny
4. please, delight
5. jaunt, excursion
6. mannerism, foible
7. imaginable, plausible
8. frugal, parsimonious
9. diagonal, oblique
10. slur, insinuation
11. pliant, flexible
12. miscreant, villain
13. prey, target
14. spontaneous, instinctive

15. discretion, tact
16. zero, cipher
17. whim, vagary
18. gloomy, lugubrious
19. hypothetical, assumed
20. traction, grip

Part VI
1. animosity, friendship
2. fabulous, ordinary
3. join, sever
4. abase, glorify
5. wrinkle, press
6. normal, singular
7. polished, amateurish
8. credence, disbelief
9. heal, aggravate
10. offensive, agreeable
11. direct, meandering
12. mechanical, manual
13. erroneous, precise
14. diligent, indifferent
15. facile, difficult
16. potent, weak
17. fraternize, shun
18. devout, sacrilegious
19. non-stop, sporadic
20. bondage, emancipation

Part VII
1. fair 2. junk 3. novel
4. converse 5. jar 6. butt
7. pad 8. raven 9. tap
10. affected 11. chuck
12. kind 13. pip 14. scar

15. vault 16. dab 17. elder
18. ground 19. patter
20. scour

Part VIII
1. able 2. shot 3. time
4. house 5. sign 6. ice
7. one 8. drop 9. fall 10. awe
11. ace 12. sick 13. pan
14. swear 15. in 16. pen
17. rock 18. port 19. net
20. cut

Part IX
1. E 2. D 3. C 4. D 5. D
6. C 7. D 8. C 9. B 10. D

Part X
1. E. 42 2. C. 40mph
3. D. 25 mins 4. C. 3 5. B. 58
6. A. Jim 7. E. 5050
8. C. £13 9. C. 17 10. A. 5

✳TOTAL SCORE✳

 80-100 AVERAGE
101-130 GOOD
131-160 VERY GOOD
161-200 EXCEPTIONAL

TEST TWO

Test Two

Part I is a series of 20 questions designed to test your ability in collecting together objects or ideas that belong to a set or that have some common attribute. To make this classification simpler, we have put together a series of words and you have to spot the 'odd one out'. There are five words and only four of them have a common theme; underline the <u>odd one</u>.

Example: bag, basket, <u>hat</u>, pocket, bucket
Answer: <u>hat</u>; the other four are used for carrying things

You have 10 minutes to complete the 20 questions.

Each correct answer scores one point.

8-10	AVERAGE
11-13	GOOD
14-16	VERY GOOD
17-20	EXCEPTIONAL

1. toddler, lad, child, infant, babe
2. pier, jetty, quay, port, wharf
3. glue, gum, tape, paste, cement
4. author, narrator, columnist, scribe, essayist
5. blithe, gay, carefree, funny, jolly
6. personable, handsome, dainty, attractive, becoming
7. check, deter, finish, restrain, dissuade
8. mirror, glass, reflect, copy, emulate
9. jowl, chin, cheek, shoulder, jaw
10. equivocate, prevaricate, withdraw, hedge, pussyfoot
11. unpleasant, conceited, ostentatious, arrogant, swaggering
12. harass, annoy, hound, harry, badger
13. abjure, repudiate, recant, capitulate, disavow
14. apathy, torpor, inertia, indolence, idleness
15. invent, fabricate, concoct, discover, feign
16. raven, jet, sable, hazel, ebony
17. elevate, increase, raise, lift, hoist
18. drowse, slumber, catnap, snore, doze
19. affirm, accuse, declare, testify, assert
20. marshal, surround, activate, mobilize, rally

Test Two

Part II is a series of 20 questions designed to test your knowledge of language and your ability to spot words that have the same meaning. We have grouped together five words, and from them you have to underline the <u>word</u> that means the same or that has the closest meaning to the KEY word.

Example: ANGULAR (blunt, stiff, abrupt, <u>branching</u>, cornered)
Answer: <u>branching</u> is the word closest in meaning to the KEY word, ANGULAR

You have 10 minutes to complete the 20 questions.

Each correct answer scores one point.

8-10	AVERAGE
11-13	GOOD
14-16	VERY GOOD
17-20	EXCEPTIONAL

SYNONYMS

1. MALEVOLENT (ill-informed, hostile, destitute, sympathetic, foolhardy)
2. UNDRESS (pare, skimp, doff, discover, deprive)
3. HUE (uproar, hunt, paint, tincture, furore)
4. URN (wise, vase, tea, pottery, acquire)
5. PERSONNEL (management, employees, departments, public, menials)
6. LEGATEE (decree, plaintiff, deed, beneficiary, garnishee)
7. COIL (string, turn, rotate, fibre, twist)
8. PRECOCIOUS (cheeky, rapacious, advanced, obvious, perceptive)
9. SCRABBLE (clamber, words, muddle, crossword, pattern)
10. CONGENIAL (compatible, fit, natural, married, happy)
11. MAGISTERIAL (correct, humble, grand, masterly, authoritative)
12. LITANY (culture, lawsuit, dispute, prayer, bookish)
13. SWEAR (imprecate, implode, impinge, impel, impeach)
14. TESTIMONIAL (investigation, deed, maxim, recommendation, covenant)
15. WHET (aqueous, stimulate, subdue, swallow, trickle)
16. DOGGED (indefatigable, foolish, irresolute, opinionated, menial)
17. WONT (desire, shortage, distress, custom, refusal)
18. DOCTRINE (document, belief, certificate, physician, theory)
19. PERMEABLE (tolerant, friendly, chargeable, strict, porous)
20. THEOREM (plan, experiment, formula, cure, subject)

Part III is a series of 20 questions designed to test your knowledge of language and your ability to visualize opposite meanings quickly. We have grouped together five words, and from them you have to underline the <u>word</u> that means the opposite or is as nearly as possible opposite in meaning to the KEY word.

Example: CARELESS (exact, <u>heedful,</u> strict, anxious, dutiful)
Answer: <u>heedful</u> is the word that means the opposite of the KEY word CARELESS

You have 10 minutes to complete the 20 questions.

Each correct answer scores one point.

8-10	AVERAGE
11-13	GOOD
14-16	VERY GOOD
17-20	EXCEPTIONAL

ANTONYMS

1. CULPRIT (witness, victim, accused, judge, jury)
2. ALIVE (asleep, inanimate, unconscious, comatose, still)
3. WRATH (choler, delight, solace, peace, open)
4. LETHAL (playful, meagre, forgiving, safe, virulent)
5. RESEMBLANCE (variation, counterpart, analogy, appearance, disguise)
6. LUXURIANT (small, barren, Corinthian, ghastly, decaying)
7. MITIGATE (loosen, cherish, palliate, release, aggravate)
8. REQUISITE (unreliable, dispensable, inappropriate, random, chaotic)
9. PAUCITY (slimness, progress, opulence, fun, sparsity)
10. TRANSITORY (absent, timeless, audacious, quickly, long)
11. GRADUAL (successive, endless, flat, piecemeal, instantaneous)
12. RECALCITRANT (bright, submissive, wilful, refractory, sociable)
13. ILLUSTRIOUS (fictitious, dark, fallacious, sinister, unknown)
14. CATHOLIC (agnostic, limited, eclectic, dishonest, defiled)
15. IGNOMINY (pleasure, honour, knowledge, stigma, wisdom)
16. DISPARATE (prudent, diverse, enlist, alike, vital)
17. WORKABLE (possible, relaxed, inconceivable, playful, slipshod)
18. STIMULATING (humdrum, calm, depressing, serene, galvanic)
19. EXOTIC (inexpensive, unfamiliar, poor, conventional, cold)
20. SLOTH (zest, disciplined, upsurge, interest, fresh)

Part IV is a series of 20 questions designed to test your ability to visualize relationships between various objects and ideas. We have grouped together five words, one of which will pair up with the KEY word to produce a similar relationship to the two-word example. Underline the <u>word</u> that is appropriate.

Example: TIRED is to work as
HAPPY is to (sleep, rest, <u>success</u>, exercise, eating)

Answer: <u>success</u> has a similar relationship to HAPPY as work has to TIRED

You have 10 minutes to complete the 20 questions.

Each correct answer scores one point.

8-10 AVERAGE   11-13 GOOD
14-16 VERY GOOD   17-20 EXCEPTIONAL

ANALOGY

1. PROWESS is to strength as
GUMPTION is to (skill, bravery, initiative, fortitude, chivalry)
2. FORSAKE is to forsook as
BLOW is to (blown, blew, blowing, blowy, blower)
3. MOBSTER is to gangster as
BRIGAND is to (desperado, bandit, fugitive, miscreant, suspect)
4. HUMILIATE is to shame as
DEMEAN is to (embarrass, mortify, chagrin, ashame, annoy)

5. LEER is to lust as
   SCOWL is to (glance, embarrassment, glower, sorrow, anger)
6. PROCLAIM is to announce as
   ALLEGE is to (explain, utter, claim, propound, predicate)
7. GLUTTONY is to sin as
   CHARITY is to (altruism, virtue, philanthropy, love, giving)
8. HOSTILE is to peaceful as
   ACQUIESCE is to (resist, forfeit, ignore, comply, dry)
9. CLAVIER is to piano as
   TAMBOUR is to (percussion, drum, xylophone, accordion, woodwind)
10. BRUIN is to bear as
    REYNARD is to (hare, rabbit, deer, fox, rat)
11. EMBARK is to venture as
    INAUGURATE is to (speech, introduce, discuss, develop, broach)
12. GRAM is to weight as
    KNOT is to (water, speed, rope, energy, power)
13. UNESCO is to united as
    RAM is to (refer, repeat, random, read, computer)
14. BLUBBER is to sob as
    ULULATE is to (snivel, cry, wail, mewl, screech)
15. LARGO is to slowly as
    PIANO is to (lively, softly, solemnly, loudly, gracefully)
16. LUPINE is to wolf as
    ANGUINE is to (ass, squirrel, hyena, goat, snake)
17. COCHLEA is to ear as
    CEREBELLUM is to (brain, heart, eye, nose, stomach)
18. RECOMMEND is to reject as
    RECURRENT is to (jam, dismiss, cyclical, vital, isolated)
19. PEDICEL is to stalk as
    COROLLA is to (petals, flower, nectary, style, stamen)
20. QUADRUPED is to animal as
    QUATRAIN is to (ship, children, volume, verse, year)

Test Two
PART V

Part V is a series of 20 questions designed to test your knowledge of language and your ability to recognize quickly words of similar meanings. There are six words in each question and you have to find a pair of words that have similar meanings. Underline the <u>two words</u> that you believe to be the closest in meaning.

Example: <u>walk</u>, run, drive, <u>stroll</u>, fly, sit
Answer: <u>walk</u> and <u>stroll</u> are the two words in the list that are the closest in meaning

You have 10 minutes to complete the 20 questions.

Each correct answer scores one point.

8-10	AVERAGE
11-13	GOOD
14-16	VERY GOOD
17-20	EXCEPTIONAL

1. remit, forget, offer, allow, bid, steal
2. jettison, reclaim, seek, discover, salvage, allege
3. destroy, debate, negate, propose, condemn, invalidate
4. exceed, exult, acclaim, laugh, cavort, rejoice
5. fresh, hygienic, lucid, unctuous, damp, sanitary
6. hereafter, herewith, hence, whether, but, therefore
7. psychotic, mentor, elder, guru, genius, friend
8. pivot, shell, kernel, corolla, fruit, seed
9. sincerity, union, franchise, goods, privilege, wealth
10. strange, insular, angry, kind, aloof, protected
11. collect, repast, goods, retort, retrace, food
12. friendship, husbandry, militarism, skill, farming, matrimony
13. arcane, strange, ancient, magic, obsolete, occult
14. nightdress, robe, shawl, scarf, shirt, vestment
15. water, snow, frost, ice, rime, chill
16. fusillade, decision, volition, option, rule, undertaking
17. anxious, noisy, sad, disquieted, antipathetic, silent
18. machine, method, fulcrum, extent, accomplishment, pivot
19. truth, rhetoric, style, answer, eloquence, argument
20. convert, device, transform, communicate, displace, condemn

PART VI

Part VI is a series of 20 questions designed to test your knowledge of language and your ability to recognize words of opposite meanings quickly. There are six words in each question and you have to find a pair of words that have opposite meanings. Underline the <u>two words</u> that you believe to be opposite in meaning.

Example: curved, long, <u>big</u>, <u>small</u>, broad, fat
Answer: <u>big</u> and <u>small</u> are the two words in the list that are opposite in meaning

You have 10 minutes to complete the 20 questions.

Each correct answer scores one point.

> 8-10   AVERAGE
> 11-13   GOOD
> 14-16   VERY GOOD
> 17-20   EXCEPTIONAL

1. reduce, possess, enjoy, relax, enrage, despise
2. blunt, humane, arrogant, ruthless, whimsical, hate
3. sensitive, discreet, callous, rational, prosaic, carnal
4. modest, spectacular, fallacious, snubbed, rich, distinctive
5. flat, concave, reversed, straight, bulging, empty
6. original, natural, groundless, basic, proven, infinite
7. noisy, annoyed, agitated, serious, composed, happy
8. observe, loathe, avoid, reveal, avert, contact
9. churlish, coy, plucky, dowdy, apathetic, brazen
10. never, often, sometimes, always, regardless, latterly
11. voluminous, vociferous, intelligent, coherent, hushed, stupid
12. arch, acme, lunar, nadir, spotless, wit
13. chapter, letter, postscript, epigram, précis, prelude
14. heathen, covert, illegal, loud, open, mythical
15. quarrel, propose, confuse, deplore, concur, compel
16. expensive, trite, small, original, important, easy
17. tired, unwise, unaffected, fit, weak, sensible
18. relaxed, sedentary, enticing, mobile, earthly, hidden
19. legislature, proletariat, multitude, aristocracy, crowd, parliamentarian
20. gregarious, frugal, antisocial, abstemious, lonely, adaptable

Part VII is a series of 20 questions designed to test your ability quickly to find alternative meanings of words. You are looking for a word that has the same meaning as one word or phrase in one sense and the same meaning as a different word in another sense. The dots represent the number of letters in the missing word. Fill in the missing word.

Example: breathes heavily . . . . . underclothes
Answer: pants

You have 20 minutes to complete the 20 questions.

Each correct answer scores one point.

8-10	AVERAGE
11-13	GOOD
14-16	VERY GOOD
17-20	EXCEPTIONAL

DOUBLE MEANINGS

1. amalgamate . . . . enclosure
2. a hybrid animal . . . . backless shoe
3. shellfish soup . . . . . . pink to yellowish-tan colour
4. to cut short . . . . hold together
5. baffle or frustrate . . . . thin sheet of metal
6. incline . . . . not fat
7. solitary . . . . small flatfish
8. inlet or deep bay of sea . . . . . free from damage
9. timid . . . a quick throw
10. very wise man . . . . aromatic herb
11. volley . . . . to greet
12. shape . . . . . fungus
13. tract of land . . . . secure vessel
14. pinch . . . small drink
15. wharf or pier . . . . deduct
16. cut down . . . . animal skin or hide
17. bird . . . . to fool or hoax
18. account . . . . . . sharp loud noise
19. strict repetitious training . . . . . machine
20. time of occurrence . . . . single-stone fruit

Part VIII is a series of 20 questions designed to test your ability at innovation. You are given the first part of the word or phrase, and you have to find the second part. The same second part then becomes the first part of a second word or phrase. The dots represent the number of letters in the missing word. Fill in the missing word.

Example: house . . . . all
Answer: hold

You have 20 minutes to complete the 20 questions.

Each correct answer scores one point.

8-10	AVERAGE
11-13	GOOD
14-16	VERY GOOD
17-20	EXCEPTIONAL

DOUBLE WORDS

1. high . . . . . weight
2. man . . . . wink
3. key . . . lock
4. bare . . . . . sore
5. out . . . back
6. red . . . . line
7. off . . . anger
8. road . . . . . age
9. err . . . hem
10. car . . . friend
11. fat . . . ring
12. plea . . . . song
13. pill . . . less
14. lady . . . . bath
15. mar . . . . pin
16. waist . . . . it
17. flat . . . down
18. stir . . . . side
19. rip . . . . on
20. rose . . . get

Test Two
PART IX

Part IX is a series of 10 culture-free tests designed to test your powers of logical reasoning and understanding of relationships, pattern and design. Study each display of diagrams and select the missing item from the choices given. Study the instructions given for each question.

Example:

You have 20 minutes to complete the 10 questions.

Each correct answer scores two points.

8-10	AVERAGE
12-14	GOOD
16	VERY GOOD
18-20	EXCEPTIONAL

1.

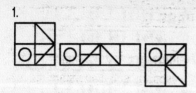

Which of the following continues the above sequence?

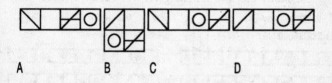

A   B   C   D

2.

Which of the following continues the above sequence?

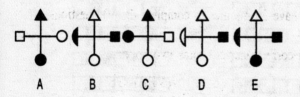

A   B   C   D   E

3. What comes next in this sequence?

Choose one from these options

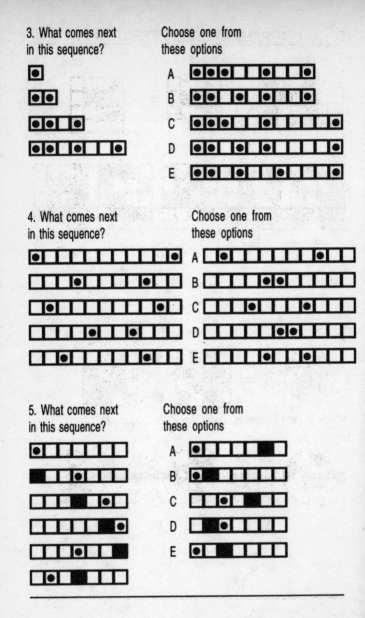

6.

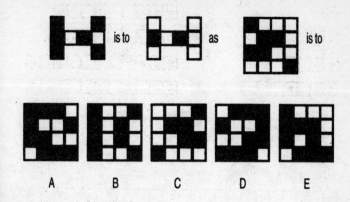

A   B   C   D   E

7.

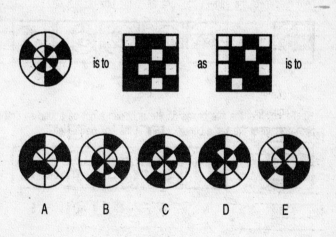

A   B   C   D   E

8.

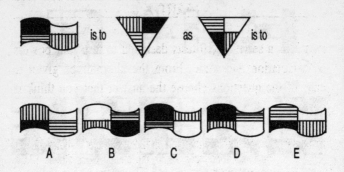

A   B   C   D   E

9. To which of the five boxes on the right can a dot be added so that both dots meet the same conditions as in the box on the left?

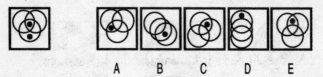

A   B   C   D   E

10. To which of the five boxes on the right can a dot be added so that both dots meet the same conditions as in the box on the left?

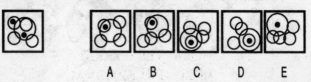

A   B   C   D   E

Test Two

Part X is a series of 10 tests designed to test your powers of calculation and logic. From the alternatives given in each of the questions choose the answer that you think is correct.

Example: My watch shows the time at 12.25; one clock shows 12.10. The radio announces 12.30, the church clock strikes 12.00, and your watch shows 12.15. The correct time is 12.20. What is the average time, fast or slow, as shown by these timepieces?

A. 2 mins slow   B. 4 mins slow   C. 6 mins slow
D. 2 mins fast   E. 4 mins fast   F. 6 mins fast

Answer: B. 4 mins slow

You have 20 minutes to complete the 10 questions.

Each correct answer scores two points.

8-10   AVERAGE
12-14   GOOD
16   VERY GOOD
18-20   EXCEPTIONAL

CALCULATION AND LOGIC

1. If a car had increased its average speed for a 360-mile journey by 5mph the journey would have been completed in 1 hour less. What was the original speed of the car for the journey?

A. 30mph   B. 36mph   C. 40mph   D. 45mph   E. 50mph   F. 60mph

2. 'What's the weight of that bag of potatoes?' asked the customer. 'Three-quarters of its weight plus $1^3/_4$lb,' replied the shopkeeper. How much did the bag of potatoes weigh?

A. 4lb   B. 5lb   C. 6lb   D. 7lb   E. 8lb   F. 9lb

3. Jim, Alf and Sid supply capital in a new business venture of £1500, £3000 and £5500 respectively and agree to share profits in proportion with the capital invested. Last year £14000 profits were available. How much of this profit was allocated to Alf?

A. £3250   B. £3500   C. £3750   D. £3950   E. £4200   F. £4750

4. Jim and Sid are members of the same cricket team and have an identical bowling average, having both taken 36 wickets for 180 runs. In the next match Jim takes one wicket for 42 runs and Sid takes 6 wickets for 78 runs. Who now has the better average?

A. Jim   B. Sid   C. Both still the same

5. Between two book-ends in your study are displayed your five favourite Carter/Russell puzzle books. If you decide to arrange the five books in every possible combination and moved just one book every minute how long would it take you (almost)?

A. 1 hour   B. 2 hours   C. 3 hours   D. 4 hours   E. 5 hours   F. 6 hours

6. Imagine two bags. Each bag contains six balls - two red, two yellow and two black. One ball is drawn out of each bag. What are the chances that at least one of the balls will be black?

A. 1 in 3   B. 2 in 3   C. 3 in 4   D. 5 in 6   E. 5 in 9   F. 7 in 9

7. A train travelling at a speed of 40mph enters a tunnel that is 2 miles long. The length of the train is $1/_2$ mile. How long does it take for all of the train to pass through the tunnel, from the moment the front enters to the moment the rear emerges?

A. 2 mins 10 secs   B. 2 mins 45 secs   C. 2 mins 55 secs   D. 3 mins
E. 3 mins 45 secs   F. 3 mins 55 secs

8. A sum of money totalling £26 is made up of equal numbers of three different value British coins. What are the coins?

A. 50p 10p 5p   B. 50p 20p 10p   C. £1 10p 5p
D. £1 20p 10p   E. £1 20p 5p
F. There is insufficient evidence to determine

9. Jim and Sid run two races over 100 yards. In the first race Sid wins by 10 yards. In the second race Sid starts 10 yards behind the starting line, thereby giving Jim a 10 yards start. Both men run the second race at exactly the same speed as before. Who wins the race?

A. Jim   B. Sid   C. It is a dead heat

10. At the end of a business conference the 10 people present all shake hands with each other once. How many handshakes will there be altogether?

A. 20   B. 40   C. 45   D. 55   E. 90   F. 100

Test Two
ANSWERS

Part I
1. lad 2. port 3. tape
4. narrator 5. funny
6. dainty 7. finish 8. glass
9. shoulder 10. withdraw
11. unpleasant 12. annoy
13. capitulate 14. apathy
15. discover 16. hazel
17. increase 18. snore
19. accuse 20. surround

Part II
1. hostile 2. doff 3. tincture
4. vase 5. employees
6. beneficiary 7. twist
8. advanced 9. clamber
10. compatible
11. authoritative 12. prayer
13. imprecate
14. recommendation
15. stimulate
16. indefatigable
17. custom 18. belief
19. porous 20. formula

Part III
1. victim 2. inanimate
3. delight 4. safe
5. variation 6. barren
7. aggravate
8. dispensable 9. opulence

10. timeless
11. instantaneous
12. submissive 13. unknown
14. limited 15. honour
16. alike 17. inconceivable
18. humdrum
19. conventional 20. zest

Part IV
1. initiative 2. blew 3. bandit
4. embarrass 5. anger
6. claim 7. virtue 8. resist
9. drum 10. fox 11. introduce
12. speed 13. random
14. wail 15. softly 16. snake
17. brain 18. isolated
19. petals 20. verse

Part V
1. offer, bid
2. reclaim, salvage
3. negate, invalidate
4. exult, rejoice
5. hygienic, sanitary
6. hence, therefore
7. mentor, guru
8. kernel, seed
9. franchise, privilege
10. insular, aloof
11. repast, food
12. husbandry, farming

13. arcane, occult
14. robe, vestment
15. frost, rime
16. volition, option
17. anxious, disquieted
18. fulcrum, pivot
19. rhetoric, eloquence
20. convert, transform

Part VI
1. enjoy, despise
2. humane, ruthless
3. sensitive, callous
4. modest, spectacular
5. concave, bulging
6. groundless, proven
7. agitated, composed
8. avoid, contact
9. coy, brazen
10. never, always
11. vociferous, hushed
12. acme, nadir
13. postscript, prelude
14. covert, open
15. quarrel, concur
16. trite, original
17. unwise, sensible
18. sedentary, mobile
19. proletariat, aristocracy
20. gregarious, antisocial

Part VII
1. compound 2. mule
3. bisque 4. clip 5. foil 6. lean
7. sole 8. sound 9. shy

10. sage 11. hail 12. mould
13. moor 14. nip 15. dock
16. fell 17. gull 18. report
19. drill 20. date

Part VIII
1. light 2. hood 3. pad 4. foot
5. set 6. head 7. end
8. block 9. ant 10. boy
11. her 12. sing 13. age
14. bird 15. king 16. band
17. let 18. ring 19. cord
20. bud

Part IX
1. C 2. B 3. E 4. D 5. B
6. A 7. D 8. B 9. D 10. E

Part X
1. C. 40mph 2. D. 7lb
3. E. £4200 4. A. Jim
5. B. 2 hours 6. E. 5 in 9
7. E. 3 mins 45 secs
8. F. There is insufficient
evidence to determine
9. B. Sid 10. C. 45

✳TOTAL SCORE✳
80-100 AVERAGE
101-130 GOOD
131-160 VERY GOOD
161-200 EXCEPTIONAL

TEST THREE

Part I is a series of 20 questions designed to test your ability in collecting together objects or ideas that belong to a set or that have some common attribute. To make this classification simpler, we have put together a series of words and you have to spot the 'odd one out'. There are five words and only four of them have a common theme; underline the <u>odd one</u>.

Example: bag, basket, <u>hat</u>, pocket, bucket
Answer: <u>hat</u>; the other four are used for carrying things

You have 10 minutes to complete the 20 questions.

Each correct answer scores one point.

8-10	AVERAGE
11-13	GOOD
14-16	VERY GOOD
17-20	EXCEPTIONAL

CLASSIFICATION

1. vest, trousers, worsted, pullover, coat
2. gin, whisky, sherry, rum, brandy
3. Spanish, French, German, Finland, Welsh
4. lemon, orange, apple, lime, tangerine
5. rumba, mango, samba, tango, conga
6. Atlantic, Bering, Indian, Pacific, Arctic
7. spruce, fir, pine, juniper, willow
8. scallop, mussel, whelk, clam, oyster
9. Holmes, Poirot, Christie, Clouseau, Marlowe
10. Lanzarote, Fuerteventura, Antigua, Tenerife, Gran Canaria
11. Chopin, Beethoven, Bizet, Tennyson, Vivaldi
12. New Orleans, New Jersey, New York, Florida, New Mexico
13. endive, shallot, courgette, wattle, spinach
14. cabin, deck, quarters, compartment, berth
15. terminus, garage, extremity, end, boundary
16. oubliette, dungeon, penitentiary, belvedere, donjon
17. patella, ulna, tibia, femur, fibula
18. view, panorama, villa, prospect, vista
19. splenetic, frenetic, irascible, churlish, peevish
20. skein, observance, gaggle, virago, parliament

Part II is a series of 20 questions designed to test your knowledge of language and your ability to spot words that have the same meaning. We have grouped together five words, and from them you have to underline the <u>word</u> that means the same or that has the closest meaning to the KEY word.

Example: ANGULAR (blunt, stiff, abrupt, <u>branching</u>, cornered)
Answer: <u>branching</u> is the word closest in meaning to the KEY word, ANGULAR

You have 10 minutes to complete the 20 questions.

Each correct answer scores one point.

8-10	AVERAGE
11-13	GOOD
14-16	VERY GOOD
17-20	EXCEPTIONAL

1. RAIMENT (gabble, garb, wet, drive, settlement)
2. KNOTTY (intricate, snarled, strangled, crushed, foreign)
3. EXTOL (curse, abandon, praise, tune, pay)
4. REPENT (advise, utter, banish, regret, write)
5. PROPHET (seer, gain, expert, designer, payee)
6. DERIDE (scrape, travel, insult, slap, manage)
7. IMMURE (shy, perfect, coop, register, large)
8. ANECDOTE (medicine, branch, yarn, deer, varnish)
9. CRAVEN (birdlike, black, stupid, abject, calm)
10. GIRD (encompass, purchase, bandage, stride, plant)
11. PAGAN (valet, printer, miser, heathen, beginner)
12. MUSE (harmonize, meditate, sing, worry, compose)
13. PROCURE (preserve, acquire, recover, relish, harm)
14. ALIENATE (turn, destroy, aid, estrange, listen)
15. MILIEU (environment, grind, fight, cold, alternative)
16. ARTIFICE (wait, shine, polish, cunning, intermission)
17. ECLAT (pastry, smack, applause, effect, catlike)
18. SUFFRAGE (pain, dotage, stuffiness, oblige, vote)
19. ENTRAILS (lingers, entrances, intestines, trenches, reaches)
20. STRATUM (stride, seam, reach, canal, straight)

Test Three
PART III

Part III is a series of 20 questions designed to test your knowledge of language and your ability to visualize opposite meanings quickly. We have grouped together five words, and from them you have to underline the <u>word</u> that means the opposite or is as nearly as possible opposite in meaning to the KEY word.

Example: CARELESS (exact, <u>heedful,</u> strict, anxious, dutiful)
Answer: <u>heedful</u> is the word that means the opposite of the KEY word CARELESS

You have 10 minutes to complete the 20 questions.

Each correct answer scores one point.

8-10	AVERAGE
11-13	GOOD
14-16	VERY GOOD
17-20	EXCEPTIONAL

1. AMNESTY (trial, amateur, penalty, home, ammunition)
2. BOTCHER (slaughterer, expert, gambler, puncture, thong)
3. DISPARAGE (praise, whip, alight, force, seek)
4. FABRICATE (weave, destroy, manufacture, hold, catch)
5. SERAPHIC (funny, salty, lonesome, mighty, devilish)
6. ATTENTIVE (indifferent, armful, swell, needful, shade)
7. AMPLIFY (shock, enforce, curtail, mummify, embalm)
8. MISSPENT (logical, busy, rich, fruitful, true)
9. WAIL (scar, linger, rejoice, hurry, fail)
10. BOUNTIFUL (lovely, nutty, high, stingy, holy)
11. HEINOUS (hideous, damned, praiseworthy, sly, hidden)
12. WRY (whole, crooked, dry, curly, straight)
13. EXPEDITE (postpone, venture, remain, pose, listen)
14. PERSPICUOUS (capable, pliable, obscure, shiny, large)
15. KNAVERY (royalty, commoner, carvery, honesty, specialty)
16. INVEIGH (support, slither, grasp, tighten, disrobe)
17. RANCOUR (sweetness, benevolence, course, calling, removal)
18. PRAGMATIC (idealistic, realistic, mundane, weak, dependent)
19. MANUMIT (scribe, sense, hurry, determine, enslave)
20. SABLE (furry, rich, white, capable, pelted)

Test Three

Part IV is a series of 20 questions designed to test your ability to visualize relationships between various objects and ideas. We have grouped together five words, one of which will pair up with the KEY word to produce a similar relationship to the two-word example. Underline the word that is appropriate.

Example: TIRED is to work as
HAPPY is to (sleep, rest, <u>success</u>, exercise, eating)
Answer: <u>success</u> has a similar relationship to HAPPY as work has to TIRED

You have 10 minutes to complete the 20 questions.

Each correct answer scores one point.

8-10 AVERAGE   11-13 GOOD
14-16 VERY GOOD   17-20 EXCEPTIONAL

ANALOGY

1. DOG is to puppy as
    CAT is to (feline, tiger, kitten, fish, claw)
2. ROD is to angler as
    LASSO is to (hangman, cowboy, shepherd, hemp, noose)
3. CLAY is to pot as
    DOUGH is to (bread, baker, banker, flour, oven)
4. POLISH is to Poland as
    DUTCH is to (windmill, dam, bulbs, Netherlands, clogs)

5. SEA is to bather as
    SNOW is to (mountain, skier, cold, ice, white)
6. INK is to pen as
    PAINT is to (decorator, colour, painter, brush, canvas)
7. WOOD is to tree as
    COAL is to (fire, miner, scuttle, shed, pit)
8. SIGHT is to eye as
    THOUGHT is to (idea, brain, plan, head, lesson)
9. DENTIST is to teeth as
    CHIROPODIST is to (nails, back, feet, massage, cut)
10. FRAY is to cloth as
    TEAR is to (rip, shred, skim, paper, talon)
11. EPAULETTE is to shoulder-piece as
    CHALICE is to (chain, medal, sword, mace, goblet)
12. RANSOM is to demand as
    PAYOLA is to (bribery, reward, wages, fee, savings)
13. COMPLACENT is to self-satisfaction as
    AUTODIDACT is to (self-indulgent, self-righteous, self-evident,
    self-taught, self-confessed)
14. FUNAMBULIST is to tightrope-walker as
    ROUSTABOUT is to (labourer, craftsman, dancer, villain,
    musician)
15. HOOLA is to hoop as
    FRISBEE is to (bat, ball, disc, dice, chain)
16. BATHYSPHERE is to submarine as
    BALLOON is to (aeroplane, space, dirigible, heavens, inflation)
17. MADRIGAL is to song as
    TARANTELLA is to (instrument, spider, Italy, dance, music)
18. BLOWPIPE is to dart as
    HOOKAH is to (snuff, tobacco, wine, foam, brine)
19. COURGETTE is to vegetable as
    GURJUN is to (flower, tree, mountain, ocean, city)
20. TURK'S HEAD is to painter as
    HAWK is to (plasterer, carpenter, plumber, postman, chemist)

Test Three

Part V is a series of 20 questions designed to test your knowledge of language and your ability quickly to recognize words of similar meanings. There are six words in each question and you have to find a pair of words that have similar meanings. Underline the <u>two words</u> that you believe to be the closest in meaning.

Example: <u>walk</u>, run, drive, <u>stroll</u>, fly, sit
Answer: <u>walk</u> and <u>stroll</u> are the two words in the list that are the closest in meaning

You have 10 minutes to complete the 20 questions.

Each correct answer scores one point.

8-10	AVERAGE
11-13	GOOD
14-16	VERY GOOD
17-20	EXCEPTIONAL

1. dream, rake, file, roué, scent, prison
2. feint, infatuate, ridicule, obsess, regret, fault
3. graphic, dreamy, forceful, rough, lifelike, petty
4. sour, rustic, churlish, citrus, clemency, leniency
5. lock, booby, pit, dolt, horse, scheme
6. dotage, wharf, saying, senility, presence, warrant
7. choose, venerate, obey, hallow, mount, emit
8. liken, destroy, impeach, generate, loathe, inculpate
9. dreamy, false, lambent, drab, gleaming, smart
10. faction, attack, furnishings, cabal, cauldron, total
11. prolix, hurried, extra, stolen, murderous, lengthy
12. easy, withered, passive, inert, mixed, reported
13. wonder, crochet, banquet, thread, tattle, babble
14. turgid, urgent, torrid, hateful, swollen, akimbo
15. slack, alacrity, elasticity, sprightliness, moving, touching
16. bamboo, limb, settle, offshoot, target, sight
17. vivify, colour, recede, stun, awaken, strain
18. music, fold, salary, pelham, grain, bridle
19. hyperbole, electrode, hallucinogen, narcotic, gazebo, welkin
20. bourne, simile, birthright, limit, extrados, ado

Part VI is a series of 20 questions designed to test your knowledge of language and your ability to recognize words of opposite meanings quickly. There are six words in each question and you have to find a pair of words that have opposite meanings. Underline the <u>two words</u> that you believe to be opposite in meaning.

Example: curved, long, <u>big</u>, <u>small</u>, broad, fat
Answer: <u>big</u> and <u>small</u> are the two words in the list that are opposite in meaning

You have 10 minutes to complete the 20 questions.

Each correct answer scores one point.

8-10	AVERAGE
11-13	GOOD
14-16	VERY GOOD
17-20	EXCEPTIONAL

1. guest, assistant, consort, athlete, messenger, host
2. invidious, confused, charitable, luxuriant, lucrative, manageable
3. auxiliary, coxcomb, chief, brigand, imbecile, antagonist
4. jocose, intimate, stingy, succulent, serious, denuded
5. glaciate, manipulate, blunt, scarify, scorch, shudder
6. messuage, largess, fracas, novice, peace, inquest
7. participant, devotee, resident, inhabitant, alien, native
8. satyr, tiro, parody, filibuster, exponent, appliance
9. malignant, solemn, garrulous, docile, benign, vituperative
10. flimsy, stupendous, cadaverous, ruddy, profuse, balmy
11. generous, agreeable, pliable, repugnant, sympathetic, approachable
12. understanding, impatience, conjecture, apprehension, mettle, cowardice
13. radiance, affluence, absolution, whimsy, insolvency, abomination
14. sanctify, prescribe, conclude, defile, purport, solicit
15. expected, selective, exalted, promiscuous, prosperous, decorous
16. occupation, propinquity, remoteness, obstruction, lethargy, misfortune
17. obesity, insecurity, humility, insincerity, thinness, insanity
18. ephemeral, eventful, harsh, comatose, dulcet, euphonious
19. anxiety, bounteous, fealty, treachery, loutish, garish
20. weakness, ignominy, sanity, promptitude, impulse, honour

Part VII is a series of 20 questions designed to test your ability quickly to find alternative meanings of words. You are looking for a word that has the same meaning as one word or phrase in one sense and the same meaning as a different word in another sense. The dots represent the number of letters in the missing word. Fill in the missing word.

Example: breathes heavily . . . . . underclothes
Answer: pants

You have 20 minutes to complete the 20 questions.

Each correct answer scores one point.

8-10	AVERAGE
11-13	GOOD
14-16	VERY GOOD
17-20	EXCEPTIONAL

DOUBLE MEANINGS

1. harsh . . . . . part of a ship
2. confused din . . . . . . bat
3. part of a castle . . . . support
4. messenger . . . . . . announce
5. scold . . . horse
6. small hut . . . . . emit
7. dais . . . . . endure
8. pause . . . . buttress
9. book . . . . . . dimensions
10. add up . . . . . nobleman
11. droop . . . . banner
12. release . . . . lavish
13. periodical . . . . ammunition store
14. composed . . . . invalid
15. aviator . . . . . steer
16. tree . . . . desire
17. pillage . . . . coarse bag
18. ascend . . . . . flake
19. compunction . . . . ancient coin
20. nimble . . . . . armada

Part VIII is a series of 20 questions designed to test your ability at innovation. You are given the first part of the word or phrase, and you have to find the second part. The same second part then becomes the first part of a second word or phrase. The dots represent the number of letters in the missing word. Fill in the missing word.

Example: house . . . . all
Answer: hold

You have 20 minutes to complete the 20 questions.

Each correct answer scores one point.

8-10	AVERAGE
11-13	GOOD
14-16	VERY GOOD
17-20	EXCEPTIONAL

DOUBLE WORDS

1. milk . . . drake
2. switch . . . . fire
3. bridge . . . . strong
4. swimming . . . . table
5. hay . . . . shaw
6. free . . . . . barrow
7. shop . . . . . . dressing
8. bell . . . . . bridge
9. kangaroo . . . . . jester
10. moon . . . . . wall
11. poached . . . beater
12. snap . . . . . . fly
13. paper . . . . gammon
14. band . . . . . wheels
15. dumb . . . . ringer
16. jail . . . . call
17. forked . . . . conductor
18. mid . . . . . jar
19. machine . . . cotton
20. firing . . . cushion

Part IX is a series of 10 culture-free tests designed to test your powers of logical reasoning and understanding of relationships, pattern and design. Study each display of diagrams and select the correct item from the choices given. Study the instructions given for each question.

Example:

You have 20 minutes to complete the 10 questions.

Each correct answer scores two points.

8-10	AVERAGE
12-14	GOOD
16	VERY GOOD
18-20	EXCEPTIONAL

1.

[heart spade / diamond club] is to [diamond club / heart spade]

as [club diamond / spade heart] is to

| A | B | C | D |

2.

[grid pattern] is to [grid pattern]

as [grid pattern] is to

| A | B | C | D |

3. Which is the odd one out?

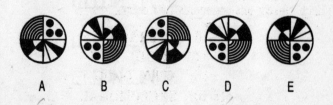

A   B   C   D   E

4.

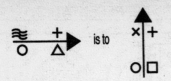

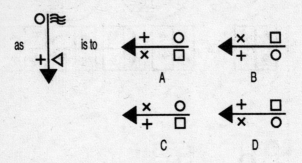

5.

LITTLE is to ⅂⊥⊥T⎾ꟽ

as MINUTE is to A ꟽ⎽∩⊥⎾E

B ꟽ⎽∩⊥⎾ꟽ

C ꟽⸯ∩⊥⎾ꟽ

D ꟽⸯꟽ∩⊥ꟽ

6. Find the missing circle

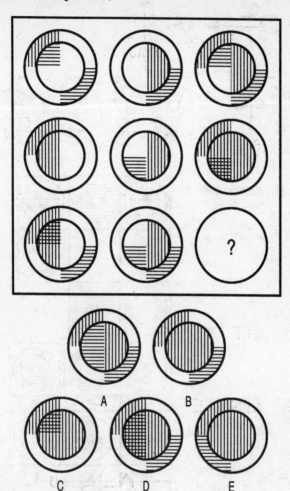

7.

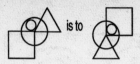

as is to

                                    A   B   C   D

8. Find the missing tile

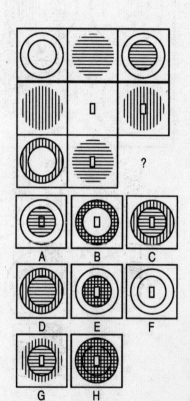

9.

as 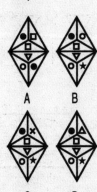 is to

A   B

C   D

10.

 is to

as is to

A   B

C   D

Test Three

PART X

Part X is a series of 10 tests designed to test your powers of calculation and logic. From the alternatives given in each of the questions choose the answer that you think is correct.

Example: My watch shows the time at 12.25; one clock shows 12.10. The radio announces 12.30, the church clock strikes 12.00, and your watch shows 12.15. The correct time is 12.20. What is the average time, fast or slow, as shown by these timepieces?

A. 2 mins slow   B. 4 mins slow   C. 6 mins slow
D. 2 mins fast   E. 4 mins fast   F. 6 mins fast

Answer: B. 4 mins slow

You have 20 minutes to complete the 10 questions.

Each correct answer scores two points.

         8-10   AVERAGE
        12-14   GOOD
           16   VERY GOOD
        18-20   EXCEPTIONAL

1. What value weight would be required to balance the scales?

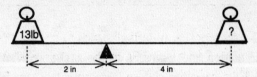

A. 5lb B. 5½lb C. 6lb D. 6½lb E. 7lb F. 7½lb

2. If 6 apples + 6 oranges cost 60p and 7 apples + 1 orange cost 52p, how much does one apple cost?

A. 4p B. 5p C. 6p D. 7p E. 8p F. 9p

3.

A   EF   HI   K ....

BCD   G   J

Logically which will be the next letter below the line?

1. L 2. M 3. N 4. O 5. P 6. Q

4. A cubic block of cubic bricks is painted on five sides. The block measures 125 cubic feet, and each block measures 1 cubic foot. How many blocks have no paint on them?

A. 30 B. 36 C. 42 D. 48 E. 54 F. 60

5. Two cards are drawn out of a pack of 52 playing cards. What are the approximate chances that they are both aces?

A. 600 to 1   B. 100 to 1   C. 500 to 1
D. 400 to 1   E. 200 to 1   F. 300 to 1

6. What does $1/3 + 1/4 + 1/5 + 1/6 = ?$

   A. $14/20$ B. $15/20$ C. $16/20$ D. $17/20$ E. $18/20$ F. $19/20$

7. A man caught a fish. It weighed $5/7$ of its weight plus $5/7$lb. What was its weight?

   A. $2 1/4$lb   B. $2 1/2$lb   C. $2 3/4$lb   D. 3lb   E. $3 1/4$lb   F. $3 1/2$lb

8. A butcher had £9.40 worth of lamb; each cutlet cost 70p, each chop cost £1.10. How many chops did the butcher have?

   A. 3   B. 4   C. 5   D. 6   E. 7   F. 8

9. The zoo had some lions and some parrots. The keeper counted 15 heads and 50 legs. How many lions were there?

   A. 9   B. 10   C. 11   D. 12   E. 13   F. 14

10. If $5 \times 8 = 44$ and $6 \times 5 = 33$, what does $4 \times 5 = ?$

   A. 19   B. 20   C. 21   D. 22   E. 23   F. 24

Test Three

ANSWERS

Part I
1. worsted 2. sherry
3. Finland 4. apple 5. mango
6. Bering 7. willow 8. whelk
9. Christie 10. Antigua
11. Tennyson
12. New Orleans 13. wattle
14. deck 15. garage
16. belvedere 17. ulna
18. villa 19. frenetic
20. insight

Part II
1. garb 2. snarled 3. praise
4. regret 5. seer 6. insult
7. coop 8. yarn 9. abject
10. encompass 11. heathen
12. meditate 13. acquire
14. estrange
15. environment 16. cunning
17. applause 18. vote
19. intestines 20. seam

Part III
1. penalty 2. expert
3. praise 4. destroy
5. devilish 6. indifferent
7. curtail 8. fruitful 9. rejoice
10. stingy 11. praiseworthy
12. straight 13. postpone
14. obscure 15. honesty

16. support
17. benevolence
18. idealistic 19. enslave
20. white

Part IV
1. kitten 2. cowboy 3. bread
4. Netherlands 5. skier
6. brush 7. pit 8. brain
9. feet 10. paper 11. goblet
12. bribery 13. self-taught
14. labourer 15. disc
16. dirigible 17. dance
18. tobacco 19. tree
20. plasterer

Part V
1. rake, roué
2. infatuate, obsess
3. graphic, lifelike
4. clemency, leniency
5. dolt, booby
6. senility, dotage
7. hallow, venerate
8. inculpate, impeach
9. lambent, gleaming
10. faction, cabal
11. lengthy, prolix
12. passive, inert
13. tattle, babble
14. turgid, swollen

15. alacrity, sprightliness
16. limb, offshoot
17. vivify, awaken
18. pelham, bridle
19. hallucinogen, narcotic
20. bourne, limit

Part VI

1. guest, host
2. invidious, charitable
3. chief, auxiliary
4. jocose, serious
5. glaciate, scorch
6. fracas, peace
7. alien, native
8. tiro, exponent
9. malignant, benign
10. cadaverous, ruddy
11. agreeable, repugnant
12. mettle, cowardice
13. affluence, insolvency
14. sanctify, defile
15. selective, promiscuous
16. propinquity, remoteness
17. obesity, thinness
18. harsh, dulcet
19. fealty, treachery
20. ignominy, honour

Part VII

1. stern 2. racket 3. keep
4. herald 5. nag 6. shed
7. stand 8. stay 9. volume
10. count 11. flag 12. free
13. magazine 14. patient
15. pilot 16. pine 17. sack
18. scale 19. scruple
20. fleet

Part VIII

1. man 2. back 3. head
4. pool 5. rick 6. wheel
7. window 8. tower 9. court
10. stone 11. egg
12. dragon 13. back
14. wagon 15. bell 16. bird
17. lightning 18. night
19. gun 20. pin

Part IX

1. B 2. C 3. B 4. B 5. B
6. D 7. A 8. C 9. C 10. A

Part X

1. D. $6^{1}/_{2}$lb 2. D 7p 3. 4. O
4. B. 36 5. E. 200 to 1
6. F. $^{19}/_{20}$ 7. B. $2^{1}/_{2}$lb 8. D. 6
9. B. 10 10. D. 22

✳TOTAL SCORE✳	
80-100	AVERAGE
101-130	GOOD
131-160	VERY GOOD
161-200	EXCEPTIONAL

TEST FOUR

Test Four
PART I

Part I is a series of 20 questions designed to test your ability in collecting together objects or ideas that belong to a set or that have some common attribute. To make this classification simpler, we have put together a series of words and you have to spot the 'odd one out'. There are five words and only four of them have a common theme; underline the <u>odd one</u>.

Example: bag, basket, <u>hat</u>, pocket, bucket
Answer: <u>hat</u>; the other four are used for carrying things

You have 10 minutes to complete the 20 questions.

Each correct answer scores one point.

> 8-10   AVERAGE
> 11-13   GOOD
> 14-16   VERY GOOD
> 17-20   EXCEPTIONAL

CLASSIFICATION

1. Germany, England, China, Poland, France
2. cup, saucer, mug, glass, beaker
3. bowler, trilby, beret, stetson, yashmak
4. twist, turn, glean, revolve, spin
5. oboe, double-bass, guitar, violin, banjo
6. plain, stocking, purl, suspender, garter
7. date, banana, orange, plum, peach
8. beef, mutton, turkey, pork, lamb
9. Arizona, Florida, Maryland, Philadelphia, Texas
10. red, yellow, silver, blue, orange
11. tuna, palfrey, tunny, barbel, pike
12. chicory, firkin, aubergine, courgette, gourd
13. matchlock, carbine, kris, pistolet, webley
14. minuet, galliard, paramatta, mazurka, gallopade
15. snowdrop, lupin, poppy, nasturtium, lobelia
16. fustic, topaz, onyx, emerald, sapphire
17. covey, knot, punnet, string, mountebank
18. crow, pawnee, choctaw, comanche, palmyra
19. brougham, pinion, droshky, surrey, carriole
20. pinnace, currach, mulatto, felucca, coracle

PART II

Part II is a series of 20 questions designed to test your knowledge of language and your ability to spot words that have the same meaning. We have grouped together five words, and from them you have to underline the <u>word</u> that means the same or that has the closest meaning to the KEY word.

Example: ANGULAR (blunt, stiff, abrupt, <u>branching</u>, cornered)
Answer: <u>branching</u> is the word closest in meaning to the KEY word, ANGULAR

You have 10 minutes to complete the 20 questions.

Each correct answer scores one point.

8-10	AVERAGE
11-13	GOOD
14-16	VERY GOOD
17-20	EXCEPTIONAL

SYNONYMS

1. OBSEQUIOUS (servile, amusing, repulsive, mighty, funny)
2. FLORID (ornate, happy, weary, rapacious, acid)
3. GLOMERATE (ripe, swollen, misty, svelte, clustered)
4. AUGUST (comprehensive, brief, majestic, monthly, jolly)
5. DUBIOUS (sickly, miserable, doubtful, forgetful, proud)
6. BRAWNY (pressed, Herculean, scraggy, likely, fierce)
7. ARRAIGN (pelt, electrocute, calculate, reserve, charge)
8. DRAGGLE (wan, bemire, stagnant, wrapped, lower)
9. INDEED (testate, surprise, level, actually, dismiss)
10. MINGLE (roller, annoy, taint, tasteful, blend)
11. SUBVERT (upset, hone, bury, veer, cover)
12. TENEBROUS (eastern, dusky, silken, thin, afraid)
13. UBIQUITOUS (damp, horrible, liquefied, sickening, everywhere)
14. VENIAL (denied, forgivable, ignored, vetted, lost)
15. NIGRITUDE (miserly, peaceful, blackness, regret, sorrow)
16. METTLE (ore, fiddle, dial, plectrum, pluck)
17. SOLICIT (cause, invite, legal, party, separate)
18. HUMBUG (kindness, insect, birdlike, fraud, glue)
19. FLOUT (angle, hooligan, jeer, flog, fretful)
20. CRUSADER (horseman, warrior, champion, sailor, Christian)

Test Four

PART III

Part III is a series of 20 questions designed to test your knowledge of language and your ability to visualize opposite meanings quickly. We have grouped together five words, and from them you have to underline the <u>word</u> that means the opposite or is as nearly as possible opposite in meaning to the KEY word.

Example: CARELESS (exact, <u>heedful</u>, strict, anxious, dutiful)
Answer: <u>heedful</u> is the word that means the opposite of the KEY word CARELESS

You have 10 minutes to complete the 20 questions.

Each correct answer scores one point.

8-10	AVERAGE
11-13	GOOD
14-16	VERY GOOD
17-20	EXCEPTIONAL

ANTONYMS

1. FABLE (preparation, haul, history, stupidity, wrath)
2. ENMITY (love, laughter, rubbish, speciality, reason)
3. MERIDIAN (forceful, sugary, dullness, anger, fired)
4. RATIFY (calm, like, act, write, reject)
5. SEDULOUS (brainy, annual, golden, inattentive, chosen)
6. TENOR (charitable, saw, variance, oval, channel)
7. THEORY (imagination, chance, thought, fact, wish)
8. ZEAL (panic, torpor, hop, freshness, lyric)
9. VIE (guard, imprison, maintain, yield, discover)
10. LIGAMENT (bandage, splinter, regiment, capsule, mendicant)
11. ARRAY (divest, brightness, deepen, fail, reduce)
12. ASSIDUITY (sweetness, milkiness, unhelpful, inattention, lightness)
13. CIVIC (impolite, collection, rural, toughness, terror)
14. QUIBBLE (argue, listen, waver, agree, question)
15. PACIFIC (continent, hostile, serene, dry, land)
16. KEN (ignorance, catastrophe, scale, rapidity, vapour)
17. MEPHITIC (fishy, neutral, balmy, testy, neurotic)
18. FLURRY (pelt, soothe, achieve, disclose, fly)
19. VAUNT (lock, draw, imagine, declare, repress)
20. RESCUE (invalidate, bind, waver, desert, extricate)

PART IV

Part IV is a series of 20 questions designed to test your ability to visualize relationships between various objects and ideas. We have grouped together five words, one of which will pair up with the KEY word to produce a similar relationship to the two-word example. Underline the <u>word</u> that is appropriate.

Example: TIRED is to work as
HAPPY is to (sleep, rest, <u>success</u>, exercise, eating)
Answer: <u>success</u> has a similar relationship to HAPPY as work has to TIRED

You have 10 minutes to complete the 20 questions.

Each correct answer scores one point.

8-10 AVERAGE   11-13 GOOD
14-16 VERY GOOD   17-20 EXCEPTIONAL

ANALOGY

1. NOISE is to din as
   QUIET is to (gag, hush, dumb, mouth, nothing)
2. POVERTY is to pauper as
   RICHES is to (millionaire, bank, money, gold, shares)
3. KNIFE is to stab as
   BULLET is to (gun, fire, aim, load, shoot)
4. SHAMROCK is to Ireland as
   DAFFODIL is to (Holland, spring, yellow, Wales, Wordsworth)

5. SONNET is to Shakespeare as
   OPERA is to (Carmen, soprano, music, aria, Puccini)
6. NURSE is to hospital as
   LIBRARIAN is to (book, shelves, library, publisher, reader)
7. FLUTE is to flautist as
   ORGAN is to (kidney, music, ear, pipe, organist)
8. NEST is to bird as
   EARTH is to (universe, garden, dirt, fox, plant)
9. BULLFIGHT is to arena as
   PLAY is to (school, children, piano, toy, theatre)
10. APPLE is to tree as
    DATE is to (calendar, hand, number, palm, diary)
11. SPAGHETTI is to pasta as
    PUMPERNICKEL is to (sausage, cheese, meat, bread, wine)
12. COCCYX is to bone as
    KIWI is to (game, tree, bird, fish, native)
13. GIBBON is to monkey as
    KITTIWAKE is to (dove, bat, eagle, gull, thrush)
14. PEMMICAN is to meat as
    LACTOSE is to (salt, rubber, tea, pepper, sugar)
15. KIBBUTZ is to settlement as
    BAILIWICK is to (garage, office, district, prison, farm)
16. TRIPLE is to three as
    HEXAD is to (six, eight, eleven, five, seven)
17. JASMINE is to colour as
    FEVERFEW is to (fruit, herb, confection, bread, meat)
18. DROSS is to metal as
    SPINDRIFT is to (milk, pollen, wool, sea, cotton)
19. STETSON is to America as
    KIMONO is to (Egypt, Brazil, Turkey, Russia, Japan)
20. PANTECHNICON is to vehicle as
    HUCKABACK is to (metal, paper, cheese, linen, brush)

Part V is a series of 20 questions designed to test your knowledge of language and your ability to recognize quickly words of similar meanings. There are six words in each question and you have to find a pair of words that have similar meanings. Underline the <u>two words</u> that you believe to be the closest in meaning.

Example: <u>walk</u>, run, drive, <u>stroll</u>, fly, sit
Answer: <u>walk</u> and <u>stroll</u> are the two words in the list that are the closest in meaning

You have 10 minutes to complete the 20 questions.

Each correct answer scores one point.

8-10	AVERAGE
11-13	GOOD
14-16	VERY GOOD
17-20	EXCEPTIONAL

SYNONYMS 2

1. implore, retreat, satisfy, entreat, employ, deploy
2. purpose, format, clamour, style, impetus, detour
3. populace, condition, hermit, grace, pleasure, recluse
4. adultery, idolatry, gentility, chicanery, trickery, voluptuousness
5. talkative, benevolent, magnificent, tallow, polite, loquacious
6. dossier, letter, hobo, dictionary, portfolio, cabinet
7. patriarch, vicuna, misanthrope, dietician, bigot, llama
8. primly, presto, slowly, quickly, prickly, blatant
9. swatch, stride, stripe, stalk, snipe, stipe
10. virile, futile, fatty, redolent, useless, gassy
11. scabbard, shibboleth, shaft, sconce, scenery, sheath
12. tenacity, nonsense, fug, purity, fustiness, belief
13. soldier, farmer, hoplite, potter, butcher
14. learned, headstrong, dextral, righthanded, lefthanded
15. adze, apiary, axe, abattoir, acacia, apex
16. zygal, H-shaped, ziggurat, behemoth, wave, dynasty
17. torus, wing, shell, skull, beam, washer
18. demanding, alert, sartorial, tailoring, beneficial, robust
19. kewpie, magician, dwarf, giant, robot, doll
20. withershins, gingerly, graciously, anti-clockwise, obnoxiously, frivolously

Part VI is a series of 20 questions designed to test your knowledge of language and your ability to recognize words of opposite meanings quickly. There are six words in each question and you have to find a pair of words that have opposite meanings. Underline the <u>two words</u> that you believe to be opposite in meaning.

Example: curved, long, <u>big</u>, <u>small</u>, broad, fat
Answer: <u>big</u> and <u>small</u> are the two words in the list that are opposite in meaning

You have 10 minutes to complete the 20 questions.

Each correct answer scores one point.

8-10	AVERAGE
11-13	GOOD
14-16	VERY GOOD
17-20	EXCEPTIONAL

1. admired, thrown, haggard, robust, fettered, cheated
2. leaning, bathos, passion, credibility, calmness, impulsiveness
3. change, bondage, catastrophe, charter, contract, freedom
4. genteel, disconsolate, discordant, cheerful, famous, gawky
5. churlish, languid, spasmodic, choleric, energetic, masterful
6. delicate, archaic, curbed, governed, systematic, modern
7. fashion, disability, fixation, fitness, convention, fortitude
8. wandering, riotous, notable, titular, unhealthy, ordinary
9. pious, sombre, sacrilegious, protected, stern, defeated
10. weighty, mazy, niggardly, lumpy, infertile, direct
11. occult, perverse, nameless, natural, disused, determined
12. plaudit, torment, tragedy, smoothness, hissing, cruelty
13. organic, relief, enigma, qualm, bulk, satire
14. satiate, store, indemnify, remunerate, rescue, starve
15. barbarian, saviour, filibuster, employer, profligate, destroyer
16. rile, range, ascend, filch, increase, placate
17. everlasting, refined, ordinary, ephemeral, important, exempt
18. nomadic, settled, curious, doubtful, remotest, sympathetic
19. foppish, doting, desirous, slovenly, animated, disturbed
20. evanescent, permanent, just, basic, distinguished, dear

Part VII is a series of 20 questions designed to test your ability quickly to find alternative meanings of words. You are looking for a word that has the same meaning as one word or phrase in one sense and the same meaning as a different word in another sense. The dots represent the number of letters in the missing word. Fill in the missing word.

Example: breathes heavily . . . . . underclothes
Answer: pants

You have 20 minutes to complete the 20 questions.

Each correct answer scores one point.

8-10	AVERAGE
11-13	GOOD
14-16	VERY GOOD
17-20	EXCEPTIONAL

DOUBLE MEANINGS

1. pale brownish colour . . . . . . ploughed but not sown
2. throw . . . . . dark resinous substance
3. tree . . . . . carpenter's tool
4. of a wall . . . . . painting
5. small part . . . . Greek letter
6. latter . . . . . . obstruct
7. an old measure . . . . . . small cask
8. measure of time . . . . . . small
9. a measure . . . . enclosed ground
10. fallen fruit . . . . unexpected legacy
11. ancient musical pipe . . . . . shin bone
12. a bird . . . . . . a disease
13. a linden tree . . . . mortar
14. a mean horse . . . . a low woman
15. composition for voices . . . . mirth
16. bundle of sticks . . . . . . old woman
17. yellow fish . . . . small boat
18. a weed . . . . . . small shellfish
19. pastoral poem . . . . of the country
20. type of iris . . . . . silver lace

Part VIII is a series of 20 questions designed to test your ability at innovation. You are given the first part of the word or phrase, and you have to find the second part. The same second part then becomes the first part of a second word or phrase. The dots represent the number of letters in the missing word. Fill in the missing word.

Example: house . . . . all
Answer: hold

You have 20 minutes to complete the 20 questions.

Each correct answer scores one point.

8-10	AVERAGE
11-13	GOOD
14-16	VERY GOOD
17-20	EXCEPTIONAL

DOUBLE WORDS

1. kettle . . . . major
2. neap . . . . mark
3. swan . . . . bird
4. standard . . . . . . bonds
5. trouser . . . . . gang
6. fish . . . . . thrower
7. mistle . . . hold
8. whirl . . . . jammer
9. tiger . . . . pond
10. powder . . . . adder
11. over . . . . hanger
12. clock . . . . caddie
13. chin . . . tail
14. natter . . . . boot
15. arrow . . . . beer
16. shuttle . . . . fight
17. chess . . . . . . chef
18. top . . . stand
19. wind . . . . wright
20. cup . . . . . walk

Part IX is a series of 10 culture-free tests designed to test your powers of logical reasoning and understanding of relationships, pattern and design. Study each display of diagrams and select the missing item from the choices given. Study the instructions given for each question.

Example:

You have 20 minutes to complete the 10 questions.

Each correct answer scores two points.

8-10	AVERAGE
12-14	GOOD
16	VERY GOOD
18-20	EXCEPTIONAL

DIAGRAMMATIC REPRESENTATION

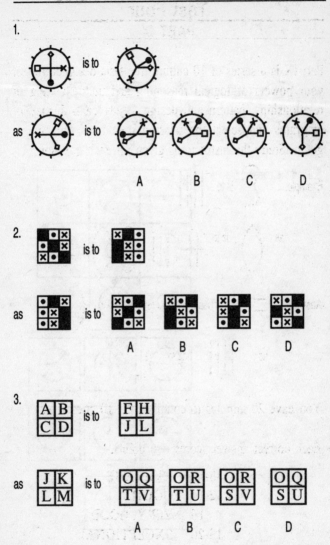

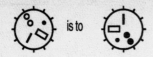 is to

as is to

                      A   B   C   D

5. Find the missing tile

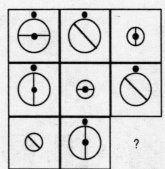

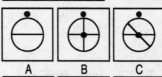

A   B   C

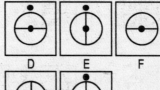

D   E   F

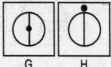

G   H

6.

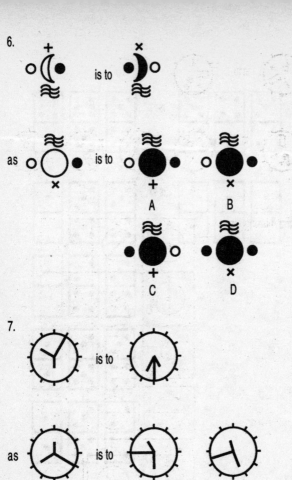

as

7.

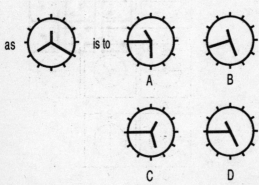

8.

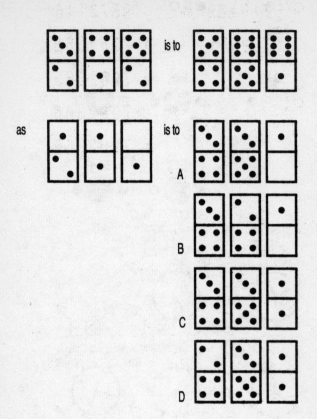

9.

6719432	is to	9872146
as 4809651	is to	A 7952365
		B 7962265
		C 7962366
		D 7962365

10.

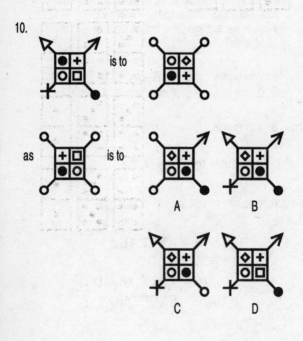

Test Four
PART X

Part X is a series of 10 tests designed to test your powers of calculation and logic. From the alternatives given in each of the questions choose the answer that you think is correct.

Example: My watch shows the time at 12.25; one clock shows 12.10. The radio announces 12.30, the church clock strikes 12.00, and your watch shows 12.15. The correct time is 12.20. What is the average time, fast or slow, as shown by these timepieces?

A. 2 mins slow   B. 4 mins slow   C. 6 mins slow
D. 2 mins fast   E. 4 mins fast   F. 6 mins fast

Answer: B. 4 mins slow

You have 20 minutes to complete the 10 questions.

Each correct answer scores two points.

8-10	AVERAGE
12-14	GOOD
16	VERY GOOD
18-20	EXCEPTIONAL

CALCULATION AND LOGIC

1. What is the square root of 14161?

    A. 139   B. 129   C. 119
    D. 109   E. 99   F. 89

2. The cold tap fills a bath in 30 seconds. The hot tap fills the bath in 15 seconds. How long will it take to fill the bath if both taps are turned on together?

    A. $22\frac{1}{2}$ secs   B. 20 secs   C. 12 secs
    D. 11 secs   E. 10 secs   F. 9 secs

3. In a horse race the odd were shown as

horse 1	4—1 against
horse 2	5—1 against
horse 3	6—1 against
horse 4	7—1 against
horse 5	8—1 against

What odds should the bookmaker give on horse 6 to make the odds fair?

    A. 2—1 against   B. 3—1 against   C. 4—1 against
    D. 5—1 against   E. 10—1 against   F. 20—1 against

4. There are 10 competitors in a race. In how many different combinations can the first three places be formed?

A. 780   B. 790   C. 700
D. 710   E. 720   F. 730

5. Town B is 3 miles east of town A; Town C is 4 miles south of Town B; Town D is 2 miles west of Town C; Town E is 3 miles north of Town D. How far and in which direction is Town A from Town E?

A. 1.4 miles SW   B. 1.0 miles NW   C. 1.4 miles NE
D. 1.0 miles NE   E. 1.4 miles NW   F. 1.0 miles SE

6. What fraction produces the recurring decimal $0.17\overline{17}$?

A. $\dfrac{17}{100}$ B. $\dfrac{17}{99}$ C. $\dfrac{1717}{10000}$

D. $\dfrac{1717}{999}$ E. $\dfrac{1717}{1999}$ F. $\dfrac{17}{101}$

7. What fraction has to be added to $1/_3$ to make it equal $9/_{16}$?

A. $\dfrac{11}{48}$ B. $\dfrac{5}{16}$ C. $\dfrac{9}{24}$

D. $\dfrac{1}{4}$ E. $\dfrac{9}{13}$ F. $\dfrac{9}{48}$

8.

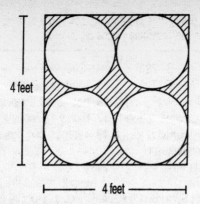

4 feet

4 feet

What is the area in the shaded portion?

A. 2.83sq ft   B. 3.13sq ft   C. 3.43sq ft
D. 3.73sq ft   E. 4.03sq ft   F. 4.33sq ft

9. How many children are there in the class if a third are under 12 years old, half are under 13 years old, six are under 11 years old and there are as many between 11 and 12 as between 12 and 13?

A. 27   B. 30   C. 33
D. 36   E. 39   F. 42

10. A man was to earn £300 and a free holiday for seven weeks' work. He worked for only 4 weeks so earned £30 and a free holiday. What was the value of the holiday?

A. £300   B. £330   C. £360
D. £390   E. £420   F. £450

Test Four
ANSWERS

Part I
1. China 2. saucer
3. yashmak 4. glean 5. oboe
6. suspender 7. banana
8. turkey 9. Philadelphia
10. silver 11. palfrey
12. firkin 13. kris
14. paramatta 15. snowdrop
16. fustic 17. mountebank
18. palmyra 19. pinion
20. mulatto

Part II
1. servile 2. ornate
3. clustered 4. majestic
5. doubtful 6. Herculean
7. charge 8. bemire
9. actually 10. blend
11. upset 12. dusky
13. everywhere
14. forgivable
15. blackness 16. pluck
17. invite 18. fraud 19. jeer
20. champion

Part III
1. history 2. love 3. dullness
4. reject 5. inattentive
6. variance 7. fact 8. torpor
9. yield 10. splinter
11. divest 12. inattention

13. rural 14. agree
15. hostile 16. ignorance
17. balmy 18. soothe
19. repress 20. desert

Part IV
1. hush 2. millionaire 3. shoot
4. Wales 5. Puccini 6. library
7. organist 8. fox 9. theatre
10. palm 11. bread 12. bird
13. gull 14. sugar 15. district
16. six 17. herb 18. sea
19. Japan 20. linen

Part V
1. implore, entreat
2. format, style
3. hermit, recluse
4. chicanery, trickery
5. loquacious, talkative
6. dossier, portfolio
7. vicuna, llama
8. presto, quickly
9. stipe, stalk
10. futile, useless
11. scabbard, sheath
12. fug, fustiness
13. hoplite, soldier
14. dextral, righthanded
15. adze, axe
16. zygal, H-shaped

17. torus, washer
18. sartorial, tailoring
19. kewpie, doll
20. withershins, anti-clockwise

Part VI
1. haggard, robust
2. passion, calmness
3. bondage, freedom
4. disconsolate, cheerful
5. languid, energetic
6. archaic, modern
7. disability, fitness
8. notable, ordinary
9. sacrilegious, pious
10. mazy, direct
11. occult, natural
12. plaudit, hissing
13. relief, qualm
14. satiate, starve
15. saviour, destroyer
16. rile, placate
17. everlasting, ephemeral
18. nomadic, settled
19. foppish, slovenly
20. evanescent, permanent

Part VII
1. fallow 2. pitch 3. plane
4. mural 5. iota 6. hinder
7. firkin 8. minute 9. yard
10. windfall 11. tibia
12. thrush 13. lime 14. jade
15. glee 16. faggot 17. dory

18. cockle 19. bucolic
20. orris

Part VIII
1. drum 2. tide 3. song
4. bearer 5. press 6. knife
7. toe 8. wind 9. lily 10. puff
11. coat 12. golf 13. wag
14. jack 15. root 16. cock
17. master 18. hat 19. mill
20. board

Part IX
1. C 2. A 3. D 4. A 5. D
6. C 7. D 8. A 9. D 10. C

Part X
1. C. 119 2. E. 10 secs
3. B. 3–1 4. E. 720
5. E. 1.4 NW 6. B. $^{17}/_{99}$
7. A. $^{11}/_{48}$ 8. C. 3.43 9. D. 36
10. B. £330

❋TOTAL SCORE❋

80-100 AVERAGE
101-130 GOOD
131-160 VERY GOOD
161-200 EXCEPTIONAL

What is Mensa?

Mensa is a society whose sole qualification for membership is to have attained a score in any supervised test of general intelligence that puts the applicant in the top 2 per cent of the general population.

Founded in 1946 in Oxford, England, Mensa has grown into the international organization that it is today with some 100,000 members worldwide.

The name 'Mensa' is Latin for 'table' to indicate that it is a round-table society that aims to include intelligent people of every opinion and calling, where no one member or group of members has special preference. In fact all its members are of equal standing within the society.

Mensa is perhaps best described as a social club, where members may communicate with other members through correspondence, meetings, think-ins, dinners, special interest groups, magazines, lectures and international gatherings, and it also provides members with the opportunity to exchange and try out new ideas and opinions.

Because it is a round-table society Mensa itself has no collective views, although, of course, its members do hold and express a very wide array of individual views. Accordingly, no one can have the right to speak for Mensa, and any views put forward, including those in this book, are of individual members and not of Mensa as a whole.

The aims of Mensa are quite simply to facilitate social and intellectual contact between people worldwide, to carry out research into the opinions and attitudes of intelligent people, and to identify and foster human intelligence for the benefit of humanity.

If you have enjoyed the tests in this book and have scored reasonably well, why not take the first step towards attaining Mensa membership by writing to one of the addresses below? If you are successful we hope that membership of the society will bring you the same immense amount of pleasure and interest that it has brought to us.

UK
British Mensa Ltd
Mensa House
St John's Square
Wolverhampton
WV2 4AH

USA
American Mensa Ltd
2626 E14 Street
Brooklyn
NY 11235

AUSTRALIA
Australian Mensa Incorporated
PO Box 213
Toorak
Victoria 3142

INTERNATIONAL
Mensa International Ltd
15 The Ivories
6–8 Northampton Street
London N1 2HY

CANADA
Mensa Canada Society
PO Box 505
Station 'S'
Toronto
Ontario M5M 4L8